SPOTLIGHT HEROES

Two Decades of
Rock and Roll Superstars
as Seen Through the Camera of
John Rowlands

MC GRAW–HILL BOOK COMPANY

New York   St. Louis   San Francisco   Auckland   Bogotá   Guatemala   Hamburg
Johannesburg   Lisbon   London   Madrid   Mexico   Montreal   New Delhi   Panama
Paris   San Juan   São Paulo   Singapore   Sydney   Tokyo   Toronto

First McGraw–Hill Edition, 1981

123456789 RABP 87654321

LIBRARY OF CONGRESS CATALOGING IN PUBLICATION DATA

Rowlands, John.
Spotlight heroes.
Includes index.
1. Rock music—History and criticism—
Pictorial works. 2. Rock musicians—Portraits.
I. Title.
ML89.R77 779′.978454′00922   80–39828
ISBN 0–07–054159–0

Book design by Harry Chester

Concept by Joanne Leslee Designs, Pickering

With all my love to Jody.
I thank you for the sixteen years you
have believed in me, and for the hour and
a half that you believed in a subway stop
at Carlton Street.

ACKNOWLEDGMENTS

My thanks to Steve Fones, Ross and Glad Rowlands, Joe Woodhouse, Scott Richards, Walt Grealis, Stan Klees, Richard Patterson, Ed Preston, Scoot Irwin, Ed Colero, Jody, Charlie Camilleri, Phill MacDonald, Duff Roman, Mel Shaw, Leonard Rambeau, Joey Cee, Stan Obodiac, Liz Braun, Steve, Donna, Lori, Dave, Lefty, and the entire C.P.I. Security team. Your lessons, interest, and opportunity have allowed me to sustain my love for music and photography to the point where I can realize my dream of this book.

Also, to Stephen Coomber of Ilford, Steve, Jeff, and Mark of Steve's Music in Montreal and Toronto, and Joanne Leslee Designs for their interest and assistance in the conceptual manufacture of this book.

And to the team at McGraw-Hill: my editors PJ Haduch and Joanne Dolinar; Herb Dreyer, Peggy Conroy, Joyce Kaplan, Roberta Rezk, Nick Monti, Bob Mitchell, Harry Chester, Anne McLaughlin, Colleen Darragh, John Rae, and Parke Puterbaugh. Thank you for the energy, interest, and time spent on this project.

For most of the shots included in this book I must share credit with my Hasselblad and Canon systems. The telephoto lens is of paramount importance in this business, and both companies have produced lenses that have served me well. Kodak and Ilford film, as well as Ilford paper and chemicals, have allowed me an optimum medium to reproduce and display these prints.

INTRODUCTION

This book marks two decades of my involvement in the world of rock and roll. It has grown from an interest that started in 1956 in my parents' backyard. A friend with a transistor radio would quiz me about which artist sang which song as they played over the air. In those days the subject matter for these tests of memory were most often the Everly Brothers, Chuck Berry, Elvis Presley, Little Richard, Conway Twitty, and Bill Haley, to name a few.

My serious involvement began in 1960 when I walked backstage after a Brenda Lee show, fully expecting to meet her. I was not disappointed. Not only did I meet her, but I spent half an hour with her, talking about everything from show business to our schooling.

Using the same direct approach, I met Duane Eddy, Bobby Vee, The Ventures, and Sam Cooke over the next year. All of these entertainers were heroes to me and the gang that I grew up with at school. Although I was satisfied doing what I was doing, I found I needed a way of verifying that all these adventures had actually happened. After all, anyone can ask for an autograph. The camera and a lot of luck "came into the picture" in 1963.

As a member of the high-school camera club I had access to a Rolleiflex camera and a professional flash unit. With a concert ticket and this equipment in hand I set out for a Gerry and The Pacemakers show. When my seat location proved so poor that the stage did not even show up in the viewfinder, I knocked on the dressing-room door. From there, I fabricated that I had traveled 200 miles for some photos to be run in a fictitious newspaper. The door was opened. I then discovered that Capitol Records actually needed some backstage photos of the band with the record-company staff, and I was hired on the spot. The photos turned out to be to Capitol's liking and I found myself involved in the early days of rock media. This was too easy ever to be called work.

The press coverage of the music scene at that time consisted of interviews conducted by disc jockeys or radio-station newspeople with limited knowledge of the act. A photograph of the artist on the local stage satisfied the papers. All it had to be was sharp, clearly showing the act.

With work from local bands filling my spare time, it was almost a year before Capitol called back with another assignment. This time they needed me to go on the road with The Dave Clark Five for a week. I accepted without my parents' consent and hit the road. I left my home and school behind, although I borrowed the school's camera equipment. Even the sixty one-hour detentions the vice-principal dealt out upon my return to school did not cool my understanding that this was going to be a fun way to spend a lot of time. I was going after this well-paying hobby.

In 1965, with a stack of names as references from Capitol, I managed to get on the road with The Rolling Stones during their first North American tour. This time the photographic equipment was mine and the week was the school's Easter break. The photos from that tour were in hot demand around the world and paid not only for new equipment but a lot of chips and gravy at the school cafeteria. Later that year the new equipment was to get tested on the group that was to change the history of popular music. I was hired to cover The Beatles both up front and behind the scenes.

Since those days, in my late teens, I have maintained that love and interest in photographing the musicmakers. They have taken me around the world to every major city from Honolulu to London. They have taken me from running for my life with The Beatles to walking calmly through a fan-filled hotel lobby with Kiss, where the absence of their makeup allowed them to go unrecognized. I've seen The Who smash all the equipment that they had onstage and, in fact, the photograph of Pete Townshend (p. 24) was taken the night The Who and twenty-three others were arrested for allegedly causing $28,000 worth of damage to their hotel suite. (It's interesting to add that Pete's portable cassette machine was playing Dr. John's *Right Place, Wrong Time* just before the party ended!)

I was with Rod Stewart when he was refused entrance to a bar because he wasn't wearing a tie and he promptly went into the lobby of the establishment, kicked over a Christmas tree, and started to stomp the decorations.

I have seen the changing times through the audiences that attend these concerts, the fans and supporters. Through it all, I have been taking pictures for record companies, magazines, groups, and managers, not only to serve their purposes but also so that I could save some of those priceless moments—moments such as John Lennon and Paul McCartney's visual reply to a press-conference question asking if The Beatles got along offstage (p. 57); or Billy Joel's reaction to a negative review of his previous night's concert (p. 121).

These moments have been locked away in images of silver that I have kept filed in my office, planning to print them up someday to help remember what it was like during those years. Each photo in the following pages evokes a particular memory. A picture of a guitarist, for instance, can conjure up all kinds of memories, since it is the guitarist who sets the mood, shapes the music, and provides us with those haunting guitar riffs that we find ourselves humming or whistling subconsciously. Who can look at a picture of Eric Clapton on stage performing and not remember the opening guitar licks from *Layla*? Who, when seeing a photo of Brian Jones with his Vox Phantom guitar (p. 27), is not filled with recollections of the music of the early Rolling Stones?

Some photos are here because of their historical value. John Lennon and Yoko Ono (p. 69) were traveling around the world in 1969 asking people to "give peace a chance" when this photo was taken. I caught Keith Moon and Pete Townshend backstage relaxing after The Who's final concert of their last North American tour (p. 142); sadly, fans on this continent were never again to see Keith in action. There are photos from the 1978 Benefit Concert for the Blind in Oshawa, Canada, where Keith Richards and Ron Wood (p. 6) and bassist Stanley Clarke (p. 135) performed as part of Keith's supergroup, The New Barbarians. Loggins and Messina (p. 84) are also captured here, backstage, during their last concert tour together.

It is still a joy for me to work with artists. The priority has changed since those early days in the Sixties, and it is now the satisfaction of capturing on film that look of emotion that is music to the eye. It continues to be fun, even though the Eighties seem to be bringing an end to the party the record industry has been enjoying since the British Invasion started in 1963. It's time to get down to straight business.

Perhaps as a yearbook is to school life, this book will recall memories from a part of the reader's life, where it touched some of these figures in music. It is, however, a book of less than 200 pages, and the photos were culled from files numbering in excess of 160,000 negatives and slides. Therefore we have tried to keep enough of the big stars throughout to make it identifiable, and yet include some of the other interesting characters who flashed in the pan, or who are just now coming into their time.

I am happy that I have seen and understood what I have about this fascinating industry. The music industry is in my blood and has been for many years. This book is a product of my interests and understanding of those individuals who, through their fans, have become *Spotlight Heroes.*

John Rowlands, 1981

SPOTLIGHT HEROES

☆ Elvis Presley, 1972 ☆

☆ Mick Jagger, 1965 (*The Rolling Stones*) ☆

☆ Mick Jagger, 1975 (*The Rolling Stones*) ☆

☆ George Harrison, 1966 (*The Beatles*) ☆

☆ George Harrison, 1975 ☆

☆ Ron Wood and Rod Stewart, 1975 (*Faces*) ☆

☆ Ron Wood and Keith Richards, 1978 (*The New Barbarians*) ☆

☆ Linda Ronstadt, 1973 ☆

☆ Linda Ronstadt, 1979 ☆

☆ Bill Haley, 1968 ☆

☆ Chuck Berry, 1970 ☆

☆ Fats Domino, 1973 ☆

☆ Bo Diddley, 1968 ☆

☆ The Everly Brothers, 1970 ☆

☆ The Beatles, 1966 ☆

☆ The Beach Boys, 1966 ☆

☆ George Harrison, Paul McCartney, John Lennon, 1966 (*The Beatles*) ☆

☆ Gene Pitney, 1966 ☆

☆ Rick Nelson, 1976 ☆

☆ Johnny Winter, 1972 ☆

☆ Steve Miller, 1978 ☆

☆ Carlos Santana, 1976 ☆

☆ Bob Weir and Jerry Garcia, 1970 (*The Grateful Dead*) ☆

☆ Pete Townshend, 1973 (*The Who*) ☆

☆ Roger Daltrey, 1975 (*The Who*) ☆

☆ Keith Richards, 1965 (*The Rolling Stones*) ☆

☆ Brian Jones, 1965 (*The Rolling Stones*) ☆

☆ Eric Burdon and Chas Chandler, 1966 (*The Animals*) ☆

☆ Mick Jagger and Keith Richards, 1965 (*The Rolling Stones*) ☆

☆ Dr. John the Night Tripper, 1969 ☆

☆ Ray Davies, 1970 (*The Kinks*) ☆

☆ Donovan Leitch, 1966 ☆

☆ Bob Dylan, 1975 (*The Rolling Thunder Revue*) ☆

☆ Gordon Lightfoot, 1976 ☆

☆ Joni Mitchell, 1969 ☆

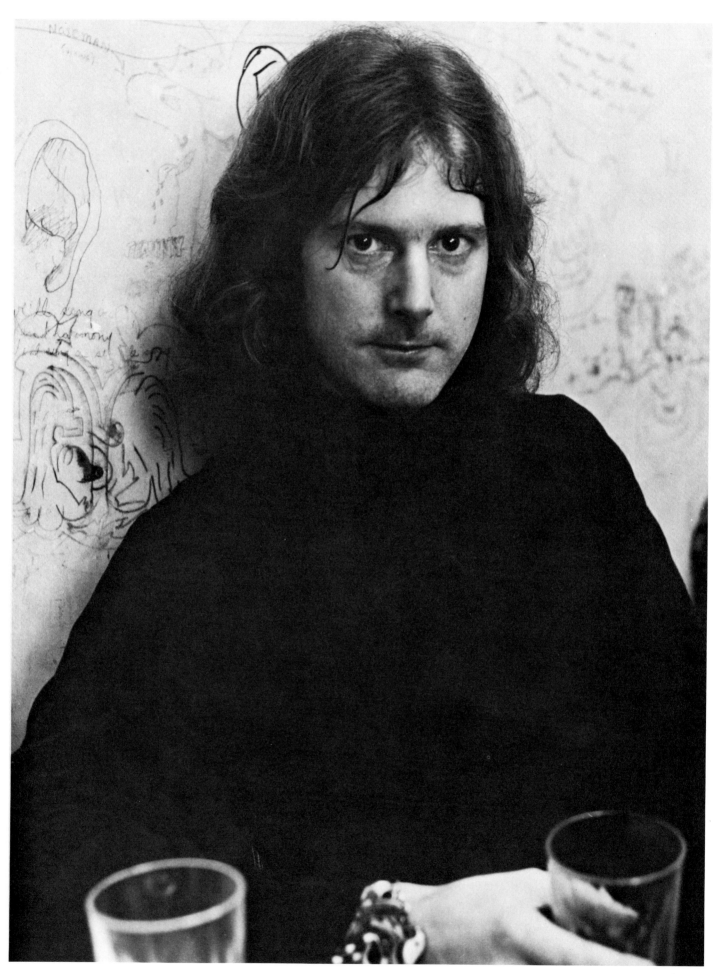

☆ Roger McGuinn, 1973 ☆

☆ Art Garfunkel and Paul Simon, 1975 ☆

☆ Leonard Cohen, 1974 ☆

☆ Janice Ian, 1977 ☆

☆ Jim Croce, 1972 ☆

40

☆ Stephen Stills, David Crosby, Graham Nash, 1977 ☆

☆ John Sebastian, 1978 ☆

☆ Cat Stevens, 1971 ☆

☆ T-Bone Walker, 1973 ☆

☆ Howlin' Wolf, 1978 ☆

☆ Al Jackson, Paul Butterfield, Steve Cropper, Donald "Duck" Dunn, 1969 ☆

☆ Muddy Waters, 1969 ☆

☆ Robbie Robertson, 1976 (*The Band*) ☆

☆ Jeff Beck, 1974 ☆

☆ Billy Park, 1979 (*Rod Stewart's backup band*) ☆

☆ Link Wray, 1979 ☆

☆ Dorsey Burnette, 1974 ☆

☆ Roy Orbison, 1972 ☆

☆ Dominic Troiano, 1977 ☆

☆ Joe Walsh, 1971 (*The James Gang*) ☆

☆ Badfinger, 1973 ☆

☆ John Lennon and Paul McCartney, 1966 (*The Beatles*) ☆

☆ Joe Cocker, 1970 ☆

☆ Van Morrison, 1968 ☆

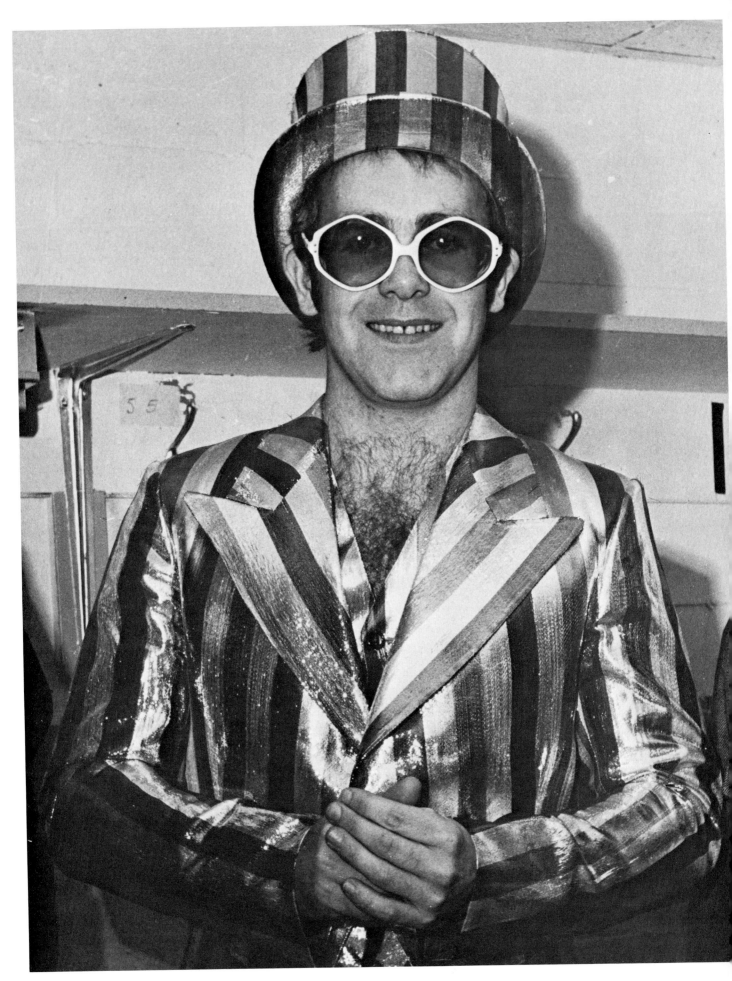

☆ Elton John, 1975 ☆

☆ Tina Turner, 1970 ☆

☆ Sly Stone, 1969 (*Sly and The Family Stone*) ☆

☆ Whitey Glan, Randy Hobbs, Rick Derringer, Allan Nicholls, 1970 ☆

☆ Marty Balin, 1978 (*Jefferson Starship*) ☆

☆ Grace Slick, 1978 (*Jefferson Starship*) ☆

☆ Peter Wolf, 1980 (*J. Geils Band*) ☆

☆ David Bowie, 1978 ☆

☆ Paul McCartney, 1975 (*Wings*) ☆

☆ John Lennon and Yoko Ono, 1969 ☆

☆ Mick Jones, 1978 (*Foreigner*) ☆

☆ Lou Gramm, 1978 (*Foreigner*) ☆

☆ Burton Cummings, 1980 ☆

☆ Randy Bachman, 1975 (*Bachman Turner Overdrive*) ☆

☆ Ted Nugent, 1979 ☆

☆ Steve Tyler and Joe Perry, 1979 (*Aerosmith*) ☆

☆ Allen Collins, 1976 (*Lynyrd Skynyrd*) ☆

☆ Ronnie Van Zant, 1976 (*Lynyrd Skynyrd*) ☆

☆ Lighthouse, 1971 ☆

☆ David Clayton-Thomas, 1976 (*Blood, Sweat and Tears*) ☆

☆ Neil Diamond, 1971 ☆

☆ Diana Ross, 1979 ☆

☆ The Guess Who, 1969 ☆

☆ Boston, 1978 ☆

☆ Jim Messina and Kenny Loggins, 1976 ☆

☆ Bruce Springsteen and "Miami" Steve Van Zandt, 1977 ☆

☆ John Prine, 1973 ☆

☆ Nancy Wilson, 1980 (*Heart*) ☆

☆ Alice Cooper, 1975 ☆

☆ Alice Cooper, 1975 ☆

☆ Patti Quatro, 1973 (*Fanny*) ☆

☆ Rod Stewart, 1979 ☆

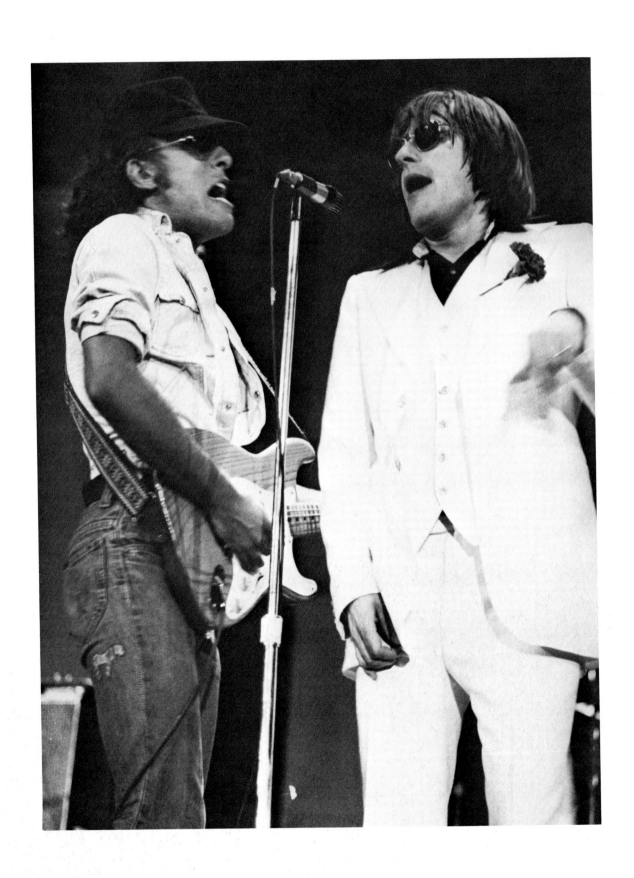

☆ Bruce Springsteen and Southside Johnny Lyon, 1976 ☆

☆ Mick Jagger and Keith Richards, 1975 ☆

☆ Dougie Thomson, 1975 (*Supertramp*) ☆

☆ Roger Hodgson, 1975 (*Supertramp*) ☆

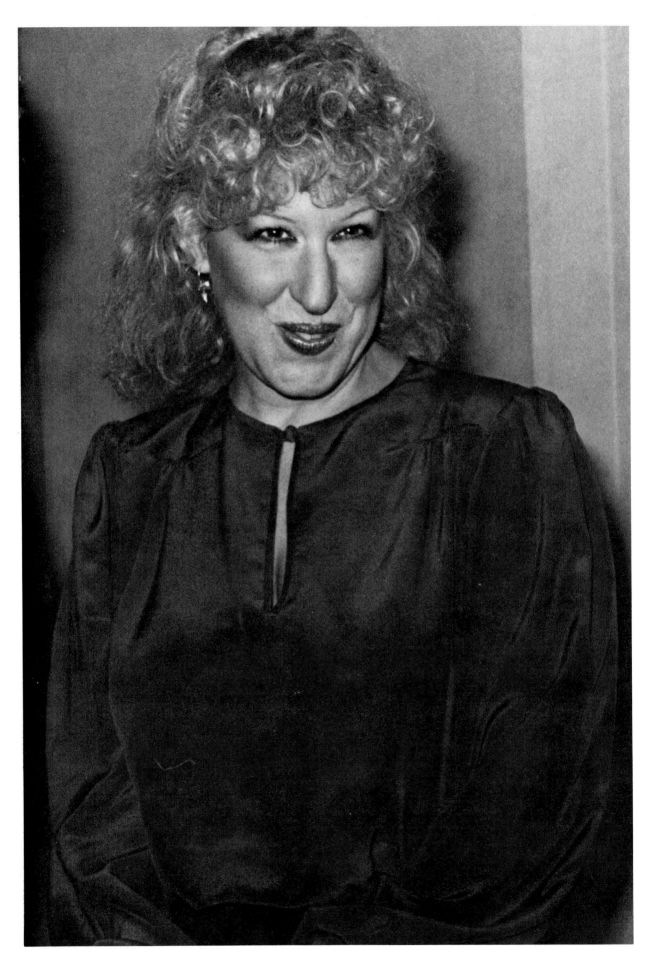

☆ Bette Midler, 1980 ☆

☆ Meat Loaf, 1979 ☆

☆ Peter Frampton, 1979 ☆

☆ Tom Petty, 1980 ☆

☆ Eddie Money and Carlos Santana, 1979 ☆

☆ James Taylor, 1977 ☆

☆ Bob Dylan, 1975 (*Rolling Thunder Revue*) ☆

☆ Patti Smith, 1977 ☆

☆ Bob Marley, 1978 ☆

☆ Mick Jagger, 1972 ☆

☆ Dennis De Young and James Young, 1976 (*Styx*) ☆

☆ Boz Scaggs, 1977 ☆

☆ Bob Seger, 1977 ☆

☆ Michael McDonald, 1980 (*The Doobie Brothers*) ☆

☆ Elvis Presley, 1975 ☆

☆ Elvis Costello, 1978 ☆

☆ Elton John, 1975 ☆

☆ Marc Bolan, 1973 (*T. Rex*) ☆

☆ Daryl Hall and John Oates, 1973 ☆

☆ Maurice White, 1979 (*Earth, Wind, and Fire*) ☆

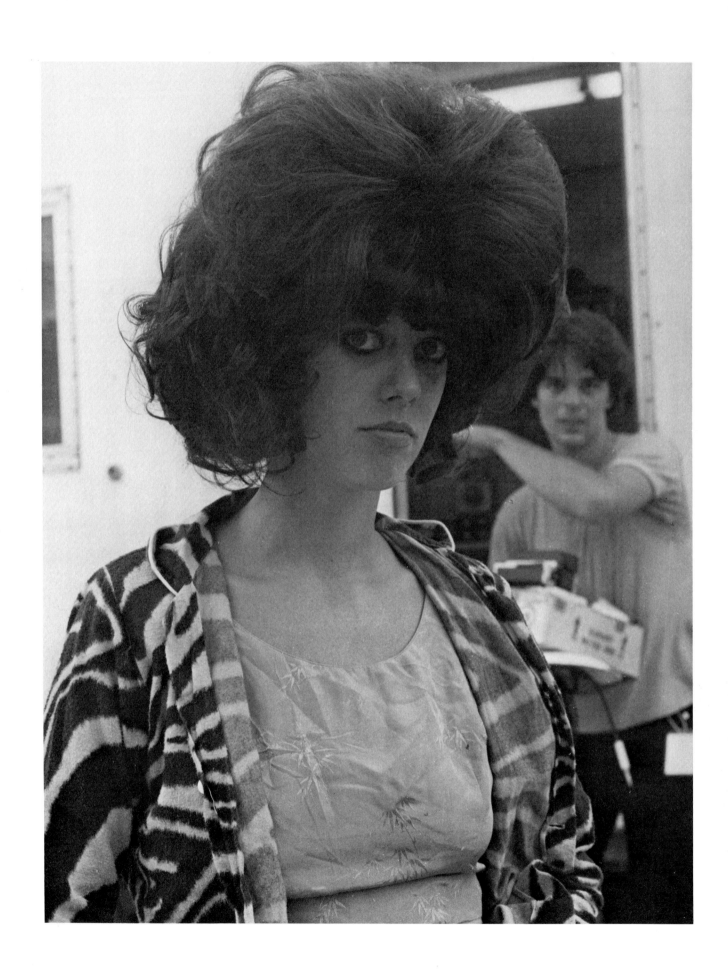

☆ Kate Pierson, 1980 (*The B-52's*) ☆

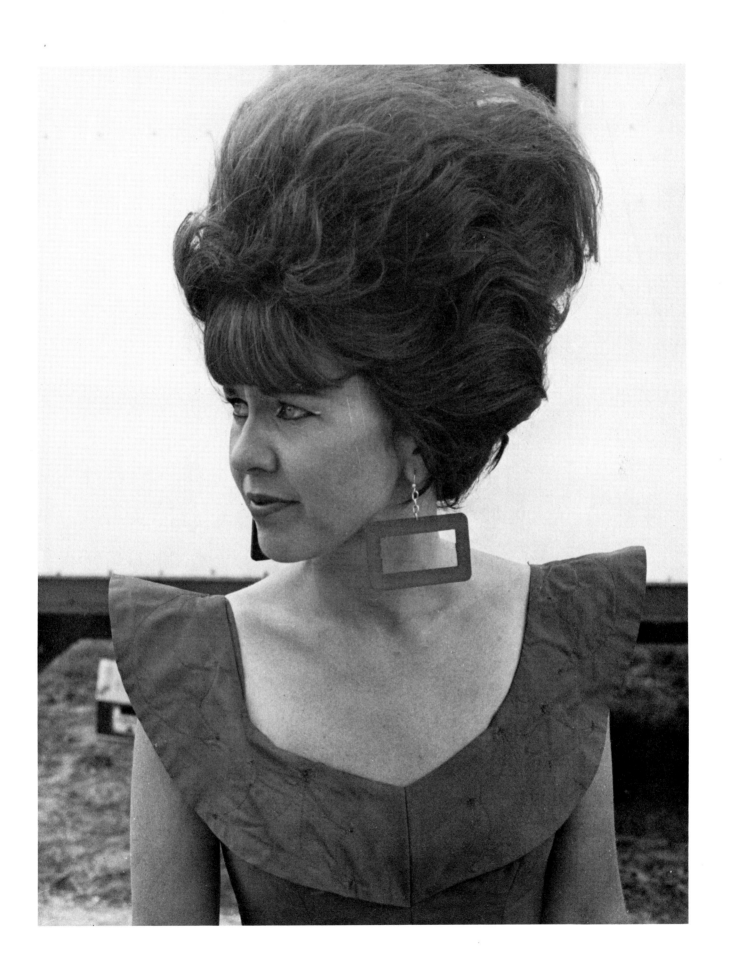

☆ Cindy Wilson, 1980 (*The B-52's*) ☆

☆ Rik Emmett, 1980 (*Triumph*) ☆

☆ Mick Ronson, 1975 ☆

☆ Queen, 1979 ☆

☆ Billy Joel, 1979 ☆

☆ Iggy Pop and Mother Superior, 1973 ☆

☆ The Tubes, 1974 ☆

☆ The Ramones, 1980 ☆

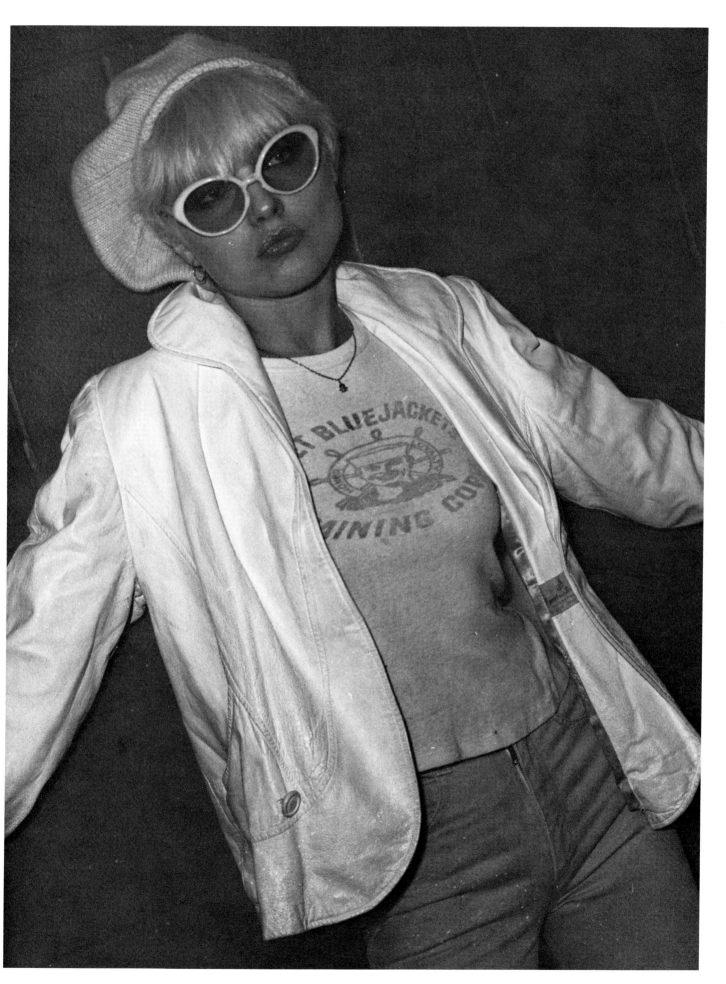

☆ Deborah Harry, 1979 (*Blondie*) ☆

☆ Paul Stanley, 1976 (*KISS*) ☆

☆ Gene Simmons and The Mighty Thor, 1976 ☆

☆ Lou Reed, 1973 ☆

☆ David Bowie, 1976 ☆

☆ Rick Nielsen's traveling guitar collection, 1979 tour (*Cheap Trick*) ☆

☆ Rick Nielsen, 1979 (*Cheap Trick*) ☆

☆ Eric Clapton, 1978 ☆

☆ B.B. King, 1973 ☆

☆ Craig Chaquico, 1978 (*Jefferson Starship*) ☆

☆ Stanley Clarke, 1978 (*The New Barbarians*) ☆

☆ John McLaughlin, 1975 (*Mahavishnu Orchestra*) ☆

☆ Jimi Hendrix, 1968 ☆

☆ Carole King, 1972 ☆

☆ Louise Goffin, 1979 ☆

☆ Bruce Springsteen, 1980 ☆

☆ Bruce Springsteen, 1980 ☆

☆ Pete Townshend and Keith Moon, 1976 (*The Who*) ☆

☆ Little Richard, 1972 ☆

INDEX

Catalog

If you are interested in a list of fine Paperback
books, covering a wide range of subjects
and interests, send your name and address,
requesting your free catalog, to:

McGraw-Hill Paperbacks
1221 Avenue of Americas
New York, N.Y. 10020